The Land of the Sherpas

by
Ella Maillart

BOOK FAITH INDIA
Delhi

The Land of the Sherpas

Published by
BOOK FAITH INDIA
414-416 Express Tower, Azadpur Commercial Complex
Delhi, India 110 033

Distributed by
PILGRIMS BOOK HOUSE
P.O. Box 3872, Kathmandu, Nepal
P.O. Box 38, Varanasi, India
Fax 977-1-424943.
E-mail: info@pilgrims.wlink.com.np
Website: http://www.gfas.com/pilgrims

Cover photograph by Ella Maillart
Cover Design by Pilgrims Publication

ISBN 81-7303-103-7

Printed in India by Gopson Paper Limited, Noida.

The Land of the Sherpas

"If ye do not acquire contentment in yourselves,
Heaped-up accumulations will only enrich others.

"If ye do not obtain the Light of Inner Peace,
Mere external ease and pleasure will become a source of pain.

"If ye do not suppress the Demon of Ambition,
Desire of fame will lead to ruin and to lawsuits.

"If ye tread the Secret Path, ye shall find the shortest way;
If ye realise the Voidness, Compassion will arise within your hearts. . . ."

Milarepa. Twelfth Century A.D.
Translated W. Y. EVANS-WENTZ.
Oxford University Press, 1928.

CONTENTS

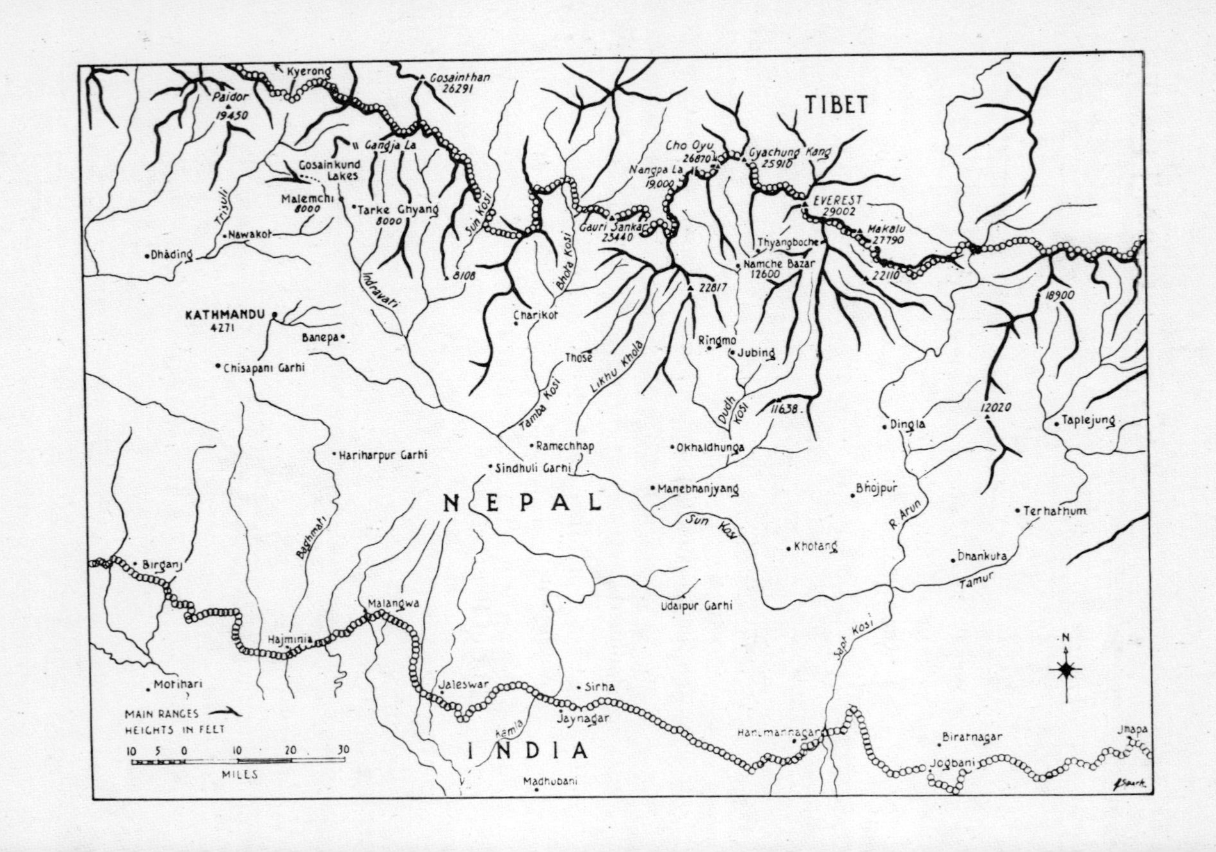
TIBET
NEPAL
INDIA
Kyerong
Gosainthan
26291
Paidor
19450
Gangja La
Gosainkund
Lakes
Malemchi
8000
Tarke Ghyang
8000
Trisuli
Nawakot
Dhading
Sun Kosi
8108
Indravati
KATHMANDU
4271
Banepa
Chisapani Garhi
Bhota Kosi
Charikot
Gauri Sankar
23440
Nangpa La
19,000
Cho Oyu
26870
Gyachung Kang
25910
EVEREST
29002
Makalu
27790
22110
Thyangboche
Namche Bazar
12600
22817
Ringmo
Jubing
Those
Likhu Khola
Tamba Kosi
Dudh Kosi
11638
Dingla
12020
18900
Taplejung
Ramechhap
Okhaldhunga
Hariharpur Garhi
Sindhuli Garhi
Manebhanjyang
Bhojpur
Sun Kosi
R. Arun
Terhathum
Khotang
Dhankuta
Tamur
Baghmati
Birganj
Malangwa
Hajminia
Udaipur Garhi
Sapt Kosi
N
Motihari
Jaleswar
Sirha
Jaynagar
Kamla
Hanumannagar
Biratnagar
Jhapa
Jogbani
Madhubani
MAIN RANGES
HEIGHTS IN FEET
10 5 0 10 20 30
MILES

NEPAL

EMBEDDED amidst the highest mountains in the world, Nepal, the last independent kingdom of India, is perturbed, for in 1949 it finally brought its strict isolation to an end. This Himalayan fortress, for many centuries completely closed to foreigners, has been an enduring example of that total hostility in Central Asia which in the seventeenth century caused the expulsion of Western merchants and Catholic missionaries from Japan and China, as from Tibet and Nepal. "First the Bible; then the trading-stations; then the cannons." Such has been the bitter experience of Asiatics.

There in the farthest corner of Nepal where only yesterday the very existence of Europe was unknown, perched perilously on the steep mountain-slopes, lives a race of gay and hospitable mountaineers, brave and incredibly hardy. These Sherpas win the hearts of all Westerners who battle side by side with them, whether when they enlist in British Gurkha regiments or when they serve as porters in heroic climbing expeditions. They have succeeded in understanding, accepting and finally sharing the dreams and endeavours of our most daring climbers. Similarly, in former years, members of the British Alpine Club influenced the Swiss mountain-folk who had hitherto refused to disturb the awful forces of nature which reign in high places. So too, when Switzerland was poor as Nepal is now, the courage of her men made them likewise the finest mercenaries of their continent.

It was the love of mountaineering which brought us our first glimpses of Nepal. This is in striking contrast to the thirteenth century, when it was on the contrary the trading spirit that revealed China to the Europeans. It was in order to sell their jewellery that Marco Polo's uncles journeyed to Peking, to the great Kublai Khan, taking their young nephew with them. In China at that time Nepal had been known for five centuries, thanks to Chinese pilgrims returning from their distant quest for the footprints of the Buddha. These pilgrims were overwhelmed by the magnificence of the nine-storey Nepalese pagodas roofed in copper and gold. It was the same Kublai Khan who, in order to control Tibet more firmly, created the first of the Buddhist 'popes', the Dalai Lama (Ocean of Wisdom in Mongolian), whose fourteenth reincarnation is today revered by both Tibetans and Sherpas.

Scientists of every description have already followed in the steps of the climbers; thanks to them, we shall soon learn the secrets of the rocks, the plants and the men of 'unknown Nepal'. One thing we know already: that visitors to the valleys of the Khumbu district where the Sherpas live call it the Friendly Land, because its people, despite their hard life, are so kind and welcoming. Their laughter is always ready; they are eager to feast the passing stranger with buttered tea, millet-beer and home-made spirits; they will dance the Sherpa Round Dance with its insistent rhythm all night long. The very name of the valley, Khumbu, is significant, for it means 'sheltered sanctuary'.

There have been some hundred and fifty Sherpas who have taken part in expeditions in the high regions of Asia. Kellas, the English alpinist, seems to have been the first, in Darjeeling in 1907, to choose a group of these men for his porters. (A few poor Sherpas had come to Darjeeling from Nepal in 1900 to find work as rickshaw coolies or labourers in the tea plantations.) Since 1935 the Himalayan Club, founded in 1928, has given certificates to these porters and special medals to the 'Tigers', those who have reached 25,800 feet. There have been many instances of the outstanding qualities of the Sherpas and of their devotion even unto death.

Indomitable individualists, these mountain people are as natural as children and their behaviour varies according to their employer. After many expeditions in their company, Bill Tilman gives them his complete confidence once 'above the beer-line'. Eric Shipton quotes one of their typical jokes: arriving at the top of an exhausting ascent, a Sherpa discovers that a huge stone has been added to his load, whereupon he laughs with as much good humour as his companions, who are already splitting their sides!

Above all, the Sherpas are affectionate and wear their hearts on their sleeves. The Austrian Tichy speaks with affection of Passang Lama, who for four months managed his porters in West Nepal. Every time they approached a summit the Sherpa stood aside, saying "After you, Sahib; your peak!"—a delicate allusion to the controversy created by fanatical nationalists about the arrival of Hillary and Tenzing on the topmost point of the globe. Tichy and the Sherpa became real partners. When eventually they parted on the platform of an Indian station, Passang did not hide his tears as for the last time he wrung the Austrian's hand, saying: "Now we both friends . . . you come back soon!" They did meet again, for in the autumn of 1954 they went to Cho Oyu and reached the virgin summit of that 26,860-ft. Himalayan peak.

Raymond Lambert, the great-hearted Genevan guide, honest and true as the Sherpas themselves, said to me recently after four visits to Nepal: "I would have very much liked to share the peasant life of the family which entertained us on our way to Everest. Their natural dignity and their gaiety are unforgettable. And there the women are truly the equals of the men, both in play and in work. . . ."

I need hardly mention the great charm of Tenzing, most famous of all Sherpas.

Yes, it is in their own homes that the Sherpas must be judged, and not as they exist on the outskirts of Darjeeling, uprooted, living as best they can, often without work, badly housed and in ill health, victims of the universal vicious circle of over-population. Work can indeed be found in built-up districts, and such work is well paid, but living is expensive and, above all, there are the constant temptations of drink and gambling.

In their high valleys the Sherpas are at home in their own world. The planes which fly over Everest and the police radio-station which controls travellers from Tibet do not worry them: such achievements are easily accepted by Buddhists whose saints are considered capable of being in two places at once, unless they prefer to follow the example of the *lung pa*—wind men—who can translate their bodies from place to place at will.

The spontaneous simplicity of the Sherpas charms us Westerners, who are so complicated and for ever at war within ourselves.

"Happiness consists above all in the balance between the world outside and the world within," said Fosco Maraini. All romanticism apart, Sherpa behaviour still forces one to recall the ideas of Rousseau and Diderot concerning the 'noble savage', the natural man whom they supposed to be born virtuous. . . .

Or is there perhaps another explanation? These mountains, the highest in the world, are believed to be the thrones of the supreme divinity. Might it not therefore be that their sacredness helps men to live a better life, helps them instead of crushing them, making them narrow and suspicious, as so often happens in lonely villages in the Alps?

I leave it to the psychologists to determine how far environment shapes men. Yet in the equally lovely valleys of the Karakoram, the Caucasus and the T'ien Shan, at the foot of the Rakaposhi, the Oushba and the Khan Tengri, I have seen Hunzukuts, Svanes and Kirghises as valiant and as splendid as the Sherpas, but without their characteristic friendliness and their love of laughter.

These Nepalese embody for me all the qualities of the simple man. These qualities touch me particularly deeply since they have meant much to me from my youth, when I met with them amongst Alpine guides and Breton fishermen. I have encountered them since in Turkestan and among N'golok Tibetans clad in sheepskins. It is a strange fact that in order fully to understand my innermost European core, I had to live in the immensity of Asia, almost at the edge of time and space and far from our particular standards and our irrepressible dynamism. Asia, only yesterday still static and traditionalist, is so vast that man, aware of his own littleness, has given first place to the divine life, bestowing on it alone the glory of true reality.

Six journeys in Central Asia had so sharpened my curiosity that I naturally wished to visit Nepal as soon as it became possible, before that superb living museum should have been spoilt by modernity.

The Sherpas live at an altitude of 10,000 feet in the eastern valleys of Nepal drained by the Sapt Kosi—the Seven Rivers. Tibetan by origin, they speak their own dialect. The region was a part of Tibet until 1856, when it was annexed by the Gurkhas of Kathmandu, who later partially freed it. From that date until 1953, Lhasa paid an annual indemnity of 10,000 *rupees* to the Gurkha kings. Even today, despite the height of the Himalayan passes—19,000 feet at the Nangpa La—it is easier for Sherpas to trade with Tibet than with distant India, a journey of three weeks to the south.

It has been suggested that Sher-pa means 'eastern man'. The phrase probably relates to the east of Tingri, the town to the north of Everest from which many Sherpas come. In the district around Khumbu the name *Kamba* is given to recent emigrants from Tibet, poor unkempt creatures who, by dint of working as peasants or itinerant coolies, will become well-to-do Sherpas in a generation or two. Sometimes they drive yaks over the high passes, loaded with the rice, sugar and paper needed in Tibet. Returning thence, they bring wool, salt, tea and religious books.

In this region of Khumbu all summits are sacred. The highest in the world, the Mother Goddess of the Winds—or Mother of the Earth according to the passport granted to the Everest climbers by the Dalai Lama in 1921—used to be considered inviolable. This Chomolungma was given the name Everest by us, after an official of the Indian Survey. Luckily it has a beautiful meaning and is preferable to many other possible English names!

For thirty years those Tibetans who were hostile to all foreign innovations insisted constantly that the Everest Expeditions would bring misfortune to their country. The offerings piously buried by Tenzing and Hillary 29,002 feet above sea-level in the highest snow ever touched by the hand of man—sweetmeats and a cross given by an Ampleforth monk—would not suffice to prevent ensuing calamity. Today Communism, born in Europe but practised by the Chinese, is overflowing into Tibet, together with its attendant troubles, in spite of underground resistance. Meanwhile in Nepal royal power by divine right has been replaced by the uncertainties of a democratic parliament on the European model. This time the disintegrating forces of our Western materialism can be blamed on ideologies and not on the usual pattern of commercial exploitation in Asia.

Perhaps because Chomolungma is too distant, the Sherpas have deified their own immediate peak, the Khumb'Ila or God of Khumbu, which looms over Kunde near their capital Namche Bazar—some sixty houses at an altitude of 12,000 feet. Khumb'Ila must never be climbed. Moreover, Khumb'Ila does not like hens, reports the ethnologist von Fürer Haimendorf, and they must never defile its slopes. There a lama may dedicate a well-groomed yak to proud Khumb'Ila, and from that moment the sacred beast will do no more work. Doubtless it will be one more symbol—like the prayer-wheels and flags—to remind the mountain people that there are things more important than the material necessities of life. Still nearer home, if there happens to be a pile of stones in the potato-patch it is worshipped as the *lou*, the god of the home, equivalent to the Roman *lares*.

Yes, the mountain is all-important and imposes its way of living on all. Just as in the Valais canton of Switzerland the inhabitants move from one hamlet to the next according to the harvest of wheat, barley and potatoes, so in summer the Sherpa cowherds live far above the tree-line, moving from one pasture to another, camping in primitive shelters, exactly like the Alpine shepherds.

Since I had decided to compare the life of the Sherpas with that of the mountaineers of the Swiss Alps, I contrived at last to obtain permission from the Nepalese government to leave Kathmandu on a five-day journey to the north-east. There flows the Malemchi Khola, the westernmost of the rivers which form the Sun Kosi to the south of Everest. The villages of this valley are inhabited by Sherpas and Tamangs: these latter also originated in Tibet, but they have been established in Nepal for a very long time. This district of Helmo is famous for its pretty girls. One of them apparently married a Sherpa from Namche Bazar who came from the famous family of Phaphlu Lama.

While I was making my preparations for departure and as if to whet my curiosity still further, I heard that the Lama of the well-known sanctuary of Bodhnath was to spend the summer in retreat near Malemchi and that the village of Tarkhe Gyang possessed an old Tibetan temple.

I must here express my gratitude to the Government of Nepal for not only granting me permission to make this journey but also, though I was travelling in a purely private capacity, lending me the services of Lieutenant Sher Bahadur Malla as escort and interpreter.

TOWARDS MALEMCHI

I SET out early in May. Climbing for three days from the 3,000-foot-high plain of Kathmandu to the 12,000 feet of the Saone Mani ridge, I first crossed huge terraced mountain-slopes, astonishing examples of the zeal and patience of the peasant, narrow strips of earth from which they had just harvested the wheat, leaving the straw standing for the cattle. They were just about to plant a particular variety of dry-grown rice before the monsoon. In the rare and isolated little farms, where I could find nothing to buy but one or two eggs, our seven thirsty porters drank a thick millet-beer which I found nauseating.

Human ants, long caravans of Tamangs in Indian file—the women wearing numerous necklaces of red beads—carried their produce: bamboo baskets one inside the other, massive planks of reddish wood, rectangular loads of hand-made fibrous paper, enormous bunches of green boughs which entirely hid the porter's body. . . .

The woods and forests astonished me in their turn. They bristled with black, branchless trunks like stumps, almost leafless, for in this region there is so little grass for the cattle that the peasants cut the foliage to feed cows and buffalo, just as they do in Auvergne in the heart of France. This habit, added to the activity of the woodcutters, is gradually killing the forest which should maintain the soil under the attack of the violent monsoon rains. As for the largest oak trees, they are burned where they stand, their trunks crowned with smoke, for their ash is needed to whiten the paper made on the spot from the bark of the daphne. This industry is so large that it has given its name to the people of the district—*kahgattis* or paper-makers.

As I went farther from these inhabited regions and penetrated into the virgin forest my happiness grew. I did not fear the bears and the leopards which made their home there. Lieutenant Malla's orderly caught sight of a big bear while he was looking for water and, the night before, two hundred yards from our camp, a leopard had carried off a goat from the enclosure belonging to a neighbouring Tamang shepherd who was camping beneath his tunnel-shaped tent of straw matting.

No one who has not seen them can imagine the overwhelming splendour and richness of a forest of tree rhododendrons—pale ivory-yellow, salmon-pink and mauve—the latter growing up to 10,000 feet. Words cannot paint a tree dotted with blood-red flowers standing out against the receding blue slopes tinged with purple by distance, under the dark indigo of the sky, whilst beyond shimmers the satin of the Himalayan snows.

One day I passed a file of porters crowned in Polynesian fashion with these red and white flowers, proud and smiling despite their hundred-pound loads. It was then that I saw arriving—believe it or not—on a man's back one of the two wives of the Lama of Bodhnath. This took place on a really steep slope full of mossy rocks which were slippery to bare feet. The matron, so fat that she was unable to walk on a mountain, had just spent three days seated on a little plank attached to a man's back by a strap going round his forehead. The sight made me realise both the impossibility of riding a mule in these mountains and the phenomenal hardiness of these barefoot coolies with their sure, dancing gait.

Eventually we reached entirely Buddhist country. With only a few juniper bushes around us, we attained the narrow Saone Mani ridge, marked by an imposing *chorten* of five storeys of dry-wall, symbolising the five elements which make up our illusory world. This religious monument with its sharp angles lent an admirable depth to the receding valleys of the vast landscape.

The wind whistled furiously as we separated to look for a remaining vestige of snow for our tea-water. The air was so cold that the spring was still frozen.

When the clouds broke I saw to the east, towards Everest, the majestic white fang of the Gauri Sankar and the chain of the Jugal Himal. To the north our ridge extended in the direction of the sacred lake of the Gosainkund. At our feet to the east gaped the Malemchi Valley, misty and heavily wooded; far to the south-east and below us I could see lighter patches which were, no doubt, the fields of Tarkhe. Directly beneath us Malemchi, our destination, was still invisible.

On the fourth day our porters returned to Kathmandu. They were replaced by a group from Malemchi: five slim young women, a lively deaf-mute and Topgi, their chief, armed with a muzzle-loader. The latter was a Sherpa, my interpreter told me, and his name means 'hardy' in the language of Khumbu. However, Topgi probably had mixed blood, for he did not have the long nose typical of the Sherpa nor the true Mongolian eye as it is seen in Lamo Doma, the charming water-carrier of Namche Bazar. He met us carrying a pair of town shoes, with which he had hoped to impress us, but a blister on his heel had forced him to walk barefoot: our relations with him therefore started with a smile! He wore the long narrow trousers and the soft cap of the Nepalese. The *kukri*, a curved jungle knife, was stuck into his wide belt. His open smile was irresistible.

Topgi took my rucksack and I followed him on the path. Soon we plunged down into the undergrowth of a virgin forest. The long descent was only too often a mere scramble from rock to root, or from dry river-bed to sliding gravel, in the shadow of fir trees or tall rhododendrons. It was there, in a small clearing, that we found a spring pasture. Not far away, on the steep slope, small cows looked as if they were rock-climbing. At night they were gathered into an enclosure of thorn bushes. When I speak of cows I mean the *dzo*, a cross between the Indian zebu and the yak, which gives scanty but very creamy milk. The watchdog, tied up, barked furious threats at us; he bore the scars of a leopard's claws.

The shepherd kept the cream which would become clarified butter for Kathmandu under his tent of straw-matting. I admired the wooden bucket full of whey in which he was swiftly turning a three-flanged churn by means of a leather thong. Thus he made a tasteless white cheese called, to my astonishment, *siri*. This product was extraordinarily like the Swiss *sérac*, which the Valaisans call *séré*, and I remembered that the Russian word for cheese is *sir*. In spite of the differences between people living at great distances from one another, here was one thread of the historic pattern which links the Himalayas with the Alps.

I was thirsty and I longed for some sour milk. Alas! all sales were forbidden on Mondays. However, the astute Topgi retorted immediately: "If you may not sell, perhaps you are allowed to give?" So, amid laughter, I quenched my thirst. The damp heat of the valley was oppressive after the pure air of the heights.

A water-wheel and two millstones close to the torrent showed that we were approaching Malemchi. Then we passed an arched *chorten* and found ourselves looking at the twenty houses of Malemchi, half-way up the mountain-side, a hamlet on a wide terrace green with fields of waving rye.

MALEMCHI

MOST of the villagers were away, camping in the forest or planting potatoes much lower in the valley. "*Ou . . . ou . . .*! Right over there!" the wife of Buru Kanche, the chief, tried to explain, pointing southwards, while I admired her handsome narrow face with its slightly slanting eyes and her wonderful natural dignity. She wore a necklace of coral and turquoise beads from which hung a small golden phylactery. When I wanted to photograph her, she put on a felt hat with fur ear-flaps. Like all the village women, she wore her brightly striped woollen apron at her back so as to protect her full skirt when she sat on the ground. In Namche Bazar two aprons are worn, one in front and one behind, at least on working days. (The apron of the Norwegian national costume, which I wore as a child, has similar gay horizontal stripes.)

Seated on the smooth earth of the threshing-floor, Madame Kanche was weaving the coarse homespun from which men's summer coats are made. Her simple handloom reminded me of those I had seen among the nomads of Mongolia, in the Pamirs and in Afghanistan.

All the houses in the village were made on the same plan. They faced south and their beautifully carved windows were built with three openings. On the ground floor was the winter stable. A staircase led to a large landing where women used to prepare vegetables. A first glance round the living-room gave an impression of refinement. Two walls were of panelled wood, with many shelves on which stood provisions and brass utensils —platters, pots, jars and wooden brandy bottles with metal bands around them. When it was cold the windows could be closed by means of paper panes, and there were also wooden shutters.

The most striking thing in this room was the family altar, a sculptured recess over the head of the low couch under the window. Before a few Buddhas, reminiscent of Russian icons in their heavy silver frames, stood the usual offerings: lustral water, rice, a butter-lamp and one or two prayer-books—large sheets of hand-printed paper carefully wrapped in silk squares.

I was invited to sit on the bed below the altar and was offered a porcelain bowl containing *chang*, a kind of beer which I do not like. But I had learnt in previous journeys to enjoy the sort of bouillon called buttered tea—coarse Chinese tea, made into bricks for easier transport, is boiled for twenty minutes with salt and a pinch of soda to help in the final blending, when the liquid is churned with more or less fresh butter in a wooden tube. If one is hungry one mixes roasted barley flour with the tea to make a ball of *tsampa*, the bread of Central Asia. Home-made spirits flowed freely and seemed to be harmless enough, for they were even given to the baby of the family in his pink satin bonnet; if it had been red, embroidered with a tiger's head, it would have been exactly what babies wear in Peking.

As I sat on the bed, covered with an orange Tibetan rug adorned with a blue dragon, leaning against a roll of quilts, I admired the room and its beautiful view of the valley. As usual there was an open fire on a stone slab in the corner opposite the window. Over it stood a tripod holding a cauldron in which hissed roasting potatoes and, as in the Valais, a square drying-rack hung above the fire. Hanging from it, strips of meat were being smoked, for the night before Topgi had managed to kill the deer which had been ravaging his cornfield.

There was no chimney, as is usual in the Alps, and this was the only detail of Nepalese housekeeping which seemed to me inferior to the Swiss customs. However, I was to learn that there was a good reason for it, for the tar in the pine-smoke preserves the bamboo ceilings and the roof from gnawing insects.

The hardy Sherpas scarcely feel the cold—any more than did the grandparents of our own mountaineers who lived in conditions so primitive that they would appal us. In the highest villages of Switzerland there are still many houses more wretched than those I saw in Nepal. I visited at least fifteen houses in all as I dealt out medicines to people suffering from abscesses, coughs, malaria and dysentery. The size of the rooms varied according to the substance of the owner, but the plan remained the same. My feeling of well-being was probably due to the happy proportions of an interior which exactly fulfils the needs of its inhabitants—as the round *yurt* does those of the Mongol—and had nothing to do with their degree of cleanliness! Comparison with the rich houses of the Tyrol, the Engadine or the Bernese Oberland would be pointless, but if one recalls the highest villages in the Trentino, the Valais, the Maurienne or the Vanoise, where life is reduced to the bare necessities, it becomes apparent that few mountain people are as well off as these Sherpas. When, a year later in London, I showed my film of Nepal, the colonel of a Gurkha regiment came up to me after the lecture. He spoke of the war in Asia and of the astonishing dignity of Gurkha soldiers in Japanese prisons. "Now I understand," he said. "They had behind them, as a part of their spiritual fibre, this perfect background. Compared with the poorer inhabitants of the overpopulated south, they are real aristocrats."

Neighbours walked in and out as they wished and gossiped with Topgi's wife, who held court as she crouched by her cauldron, sitting-room and kitchen happily combined as they are in the most up-to-date American houses. When she needed spices or another pot she opened a sliding panel. Near the door, where the tools were kept, Topgi was making a dresser; its joints were nailless as in our own old-fashioned furniture. When he talked to his wife Topgi did not use the *parbatya* language spoken by my interpreter; his sing-song speech was sibilant and seemed akin to the rich harmonies of the Tibetan and Chinese tongues. He showed me, stacked in the corner, a sheaf of daphne bark which he intended to turn into paper.

Neighbours discussed the political troubles which were affecting the hill-people. In the big town, five days away, prices were mounting and the economy of the country was unbalanced.

In front of the house a child was stuffing a red pheasant with straw; he had caught it in a snare that very morning. Outside the next house a wrinkled old woman was making a large bamboo basket as she gossiped and joked with two friends. It was for a coop to protect the chicks from hawks.

My camp was established on the grass by the prayer-flags in front of the temple. The temple roof was in need of repairs, as were the frescoes decorating the walls of the verandah where, in accordance with tradition, were represented the deities guarding the four directions of space.

My every movement was watched by mischievous, charming and intelligent children. As I put up my tent and my primus stove, they came to dip their filthy hands in the water I had just used. I soaped the supple paws of the youngest girl; after the third washing she looked at the smooth skin of her palm with delight and immediately all the others wanted to play with the soap too!

Inside the dark temple, lit only from the doorway, the sacred triad of Buddhas loomed over the altar. Nearby a cluster of blood-red rhododendron flowers was tucked into the elbow of a small bronze Buddha, a magnificent offering. Sacred banners hung from the ceiling, together with an enormous shallow drum. For the time being it hid within its hollow depth its potentialities for resounding and booming sound—a deep tone which is as moving as that of a great cathedral bell.

The next day I visited the wife of the Lama of Bodhnath. She was settling down and resting after her journey on man's-back. She was dressed in the latest Kathmandu fashion, which is to say that she was wearing a *sari*. She played with her little Lhasa terrier and told her daughter-in-law to remove the winter dust from the shelves. She accepted a slab of butter presented to her by a Sherpani in a Tibetan apron full of holes. Butter is the most precious product of Asia and is offered to the powers earthly and heavenly, the propitiatory gift common to Mongolia, Tibet and India. Accepting the offering, the matron took a pinch of it and squeezed it upon her hair in the middle of her parting—in token of consent—asking me whether I was short of butter. Thus my expedition was enriched by a pat of butter mixed with *dzo* hairs.

Later a wrinkled old man came to visit me. I showed him a photograph of the late Panchen Lama which I had once acquired in the monastery of Kumbum near the Koko Nor. In spite of his modest appearance this villager could read the Tibetan caption; in sign of respect he lifted the portrait to his forehead. Whereas the Dalai Lama is the reincarnation of Avalokitesvara, the spiritual son of the solar Buddha Amitabha, the Panchen Lama is the incarnation of Amitabha himself. The two pontiffs are of equal importance and, when they meet, the elder takes precedence. The present Panchen Lama, a young man born near the Chinese-Tibetan border, was brought to Lhasa and forced on the Tibetan Government by the Chinese Communists.

Europe means nothing to the Buddhists of these high regions. Their world lies to the north. Before the era of empty tins left by climbing expeditions—their first contact with another world—all their culture came from Tibet; their clothes—Tibetan boots with high square Chinese soles, woollen robes, brightly coloured aprons edged with costly brocade, Chinese silk dresses for the priests and for the Demons' Dances; their food too—tea, Chinese noodles, porcelain bowls with covers to keep the flies out, even chopsticks used around Khumbu; their way of worship—sacred books printed in Tibetan, silver amulets, clay-seals stamped with the symbols of pilgrimages, temple frescoes painted by Tibetan craftsmen and the stone sculptures of sacred formulas on the *mani* walls erected in memory of the dead.

When they dress to go out the women of the Helmo district wear a three-quarter-length kimono with narrow coloured revers, much closer to ancient T'ang statuettes than to actual Tibetan fashion. Each time that I prepared to film Topgi's sister she quickly folded a small sash which she normally carried over her arm into a kind of improvised mortar-board and popped it on her head.

It seems that Malemchi is sufficiently influenced by the proximity of Kathmandu to have abandoned the polyandry of the Sherpas, still practised in Khumbu and in the Langtang Valley near the Tibetan border, north of Malemchi over the 19,000-foot pass of the Gangja La. This valley sided with Nepal during the fighting with Tibet in 1856 and as a reward received permission to continue its polyandrous practices. Quite the opposite custom can be observed among the Hindus living in Kathmandu, and it is known that the father of the Buddha, who ruled over the southern border of Nepal some six centuries B.C., had two queens. Even today this custom still prevails among the kings of Nepal, and, curiously enough, with the Lama of Bodhnath, who belongs to the 'Red Hat' sect of lamaism which recognises marriage.

Now that Communism has established itself to the north of Nepal and the Dalai Lama has even visited Peking, it will be interesting to see whether pious Buddhists will turn towards the culture of the south, towards democratic and parliamentary India which, hitherto, they have only visited in order to join a Gurkha regiment for the sake of its safe pension.

TARKHE GYANG

WE continued on our way eastwards towards Tarkhe Gyang (*gyang* means temple), by a path which, although it was very steep, really was a path. We crossed the last tiny fields of the valley: their terraces so narrow that a labourer had difficulty in turning his plough drawn by a *dzo*. The rye had already been harvested and was being replaced by potatoes.

The houses that we passed had bright geraniums gaily decorating their balconies. As it grew hotter the farther we descended, I went to ask for curds as often as possible. We managed to cross the torrent on foot, as the waters were low. Nothing remained of the bridge, carried away by the last monsoon, but the original piers.

The sun beat down and burned as we climbed the hillside. Not a breeze stirred in this intense oppressiveness, so that sweat ran down my arms and legs. Frequently Topgi turned aside to a cottage "to see one of my sisters". We teased him about this, as we knew that he was not as hot as I was and preferred rice-brandy to sour milk.

Chortens stood at every cross-roads, and I saw one of particular interest at the entrance to a monastery where men, singing as they worked, were repairing the roof of thick shingles. Prayer-flags fluttered in the wind which had just sprung up.

At last we had climbed to the height of Tarkhe, which we entered from behind, seeing as we passed a group of people husking corn. This was done by manipulating with the foot a huge hammer-headed beam which hit the grain in a hollow. Another man winnowed it, holding a light straw tray above his head.

We were given a welcoming drink in a silver-lined wooden bowl by Lakpuri, another of Topgi's sisters, in a traditional room. She used a bamboo pipe to blow up the flame of the fire. The village had some five hundred inhabitants, but I learnt that many of them were away, working in the fields lower down the valley. No Babu, the headman of the village, had been a lama in Lhasa for many years, and it was to him that I told my desire to see the Sherpas' Round Dance. I had just missed one of the Demons' Dances when the enormous carved masks from the temples are worn. Masks somewhat similar and equally terrifying are to be found in the Lötschental in Switzerland, but their original significance is lost in antiquity.

As I lay in my sleeping-bag ready for sleep and looked through the triangular opening of the tent, instead of the starry sky of the Central Himalayas I saw a splendid prayer-wheel ten feet high shining with mediæval Nepalese letters in copper. A ragged old woman had just lit, as she did every evening, a butter-lamp before this cylinder full of esoteric formulas: "*Aum! Mani padme hum!* Salutation to the Jewel in the lotus!"

The village headman had allowed me to camp on the first floor of the Buddhist temple in an empty room decorated with frescoes depicting the Buddhist pantheon. All day long the paper panes of the wooden trellis windows were pierced by the fingers of children wanting to look at the first European woman to come to their village, some 8,000 feet up and the highest in that valley.

Lieutenant Malla camped on the verandah of the ground-floor with his sergeant, his orderly and his cook. Contrary to the normal oriental custom, I was travelling without a servant, for I had decided to put into practice the new democracy of Nepal which was being preached everywhere. It was for this reason, too, that I had gone to the royal palace to interview King Tribhuvana on a democratic bicycle! My intelligent Nepalese lieutenant came of the line of Malla kings who were crushed in the eighteenth century by the conquering Gurkha invaders. He could not eat with me since he had to abide by the rules of his Newar caste and his meals were prepared by his Brahmin cook. To the onlookers he must indeed have seemed the leader of our group!

In the end I had to put up my tent for protection not from the weather but from the curiosity of the villagers who, from dawn onwards, seemed to be urged by irrepressible religious zeal to come and turn the prayer-wheel—meanwhile staring curiously in my direction. I was woken by the bell which, hanging from the ceiling, was set in motion by every turn of the cylinder.

That night I found it difficult to sleep, not because of the Tantric deities on the wall but owing to the huge Tibetan mastiffs that seemed to howl all night long. Moreover, I suddenly had an overwhelming sensation that I lay at the heart of Asia at a moment crucial in the history of Nepal.

What a strange country Nepal is! Still living in the Middle Ages, it has only just opened its frontiers, and the aeroplane had transformed the life of the capital long before that town was linked to India by the road, which was only finished in 1953. Before this came about King Tribhuvana, terrestrial incarnation of Vishnu the Preserver of mankind, had made common cause with the revolutionaries in order to terminate the hereditary absolute power of his Prime Minister. He instituted universal suffrage among his seven million subjects of very various origins, living in remote and inaccessible valleys—a rather ambitious undertaking. Almost immediately there appeared on the scene all the amenities of civilisation: whisky, cinemas, newspapers, hotels, a radio-station of course, as well as a great variety of technicians, gramophones, Jesuit schoolmasters, an Indian Embassy and an American delegation—whereas for the previous 135 years England had been the only country to have representatives in the land of the Gurkhas. The arrival of a Chinese delegation has also been announced. Political parties are springing up like mushrooms and, as always, this results in disturbances. Moreover, the Exchequer is very low . . . !

The upheaval inseparable from modernisation had not yet reached the Malemchi valley, where I woke up early to notice that for once that morning there were no villagers near my tent. I heard the far-off boom of the great drum like thunder in a distant cave and the flapping of the prayer-flags, reminding the people unceasingly that real life is spirit and that the Buddha alone is 'awake'. A few children, curious and sniffing as usual, watched me as I tried to crawl out of the tent with dignity. By means of signs a girl offered to do my washing. She would go to soap it at the spring where the villagers filled their brass jugs. She would like to come back with me to Europe. She was much more forthcoming than her friends and she wore a cheap printed cotton skirt, crudely coloured, from which I judged that she had been away from Tarkhe. Following her into her home, I admired again the comfort of the traditionally arranged living-room.

Distributing medicine in this village, which was much cleaner than many I have known, I noticed that each house had a lavatory at the end of the passage and, as in Switzerland, pine needles and ashes were used to build up the manure. The girl showed me with pride a picture of General Bijaya, Nepalese Minister for Foreign Affairs, in whose house she had been a servant. He was wearing his best uniform covered with jewels and his magnificent helmet adorned with bird of paradise plumes. I had met this General in the Palace of Singha Durbar, eight days before his father, the Maharajah and last hereditary Prime Minister, surrendered that building to the Congress Party, heir to his power.

While her neighbour, Tung Sang Lamini, drew on her water-pipe, the girl prepared tea for me, still hoping that I would take her into my service. Tung Sang Lamini was a widow who had once been to Rangoon to visit her brother, priest in a Burmese pagoda. I heard how her life had been saved when the Japanese machine-gunned the people escaping towards India. Some soldiers stopped her to find out what she was carrying so carefully wrapped in a cloth. When they discovered that she was sister to a priest and was starting on a three months' flight with nothing but the sacred book of the Prajnaparamita—Transcendent Knowledge—they gave her a safe conduct.

I also visited No Babu, who wanted me to see his sick mother. I found the old lady next door on a pile of furs on the floor. She looked both formidable and intelligent. I learned that she had had dysentery for three months. Her first attack had been soon after she had taken a hot bath and oiled herself "in the usual way". Such clean customs in such a place astonished me.

I set off to explore through narrow streets between stone houses with shingled roofs. Only the prayer-flags reminded me that I was not in the Alps. At the back entrance to the village, where the path suddenly emerged from the depths of the valley, a solitary child was placing carefully on the ground some strange object which surely was not a toy. It looked like a tray with doll-like figures on horseback—the whole thing modelled out of a brownish dough. I discovered later that the father of this child Naropa, bedridden for three months, had just been exorcised; thanks to the magic of this same tray the illness was banished from the village.

At the beginning of my stay I might have thought that these people lived like European mountaineers, minding their cattle, making butter and cultivating their fields. But I was beginning to guess that they lead a life on two levels. In what concerns their religious thought they deal with a subtle world where care must constantly be taken to propitiate invisible forces, those tutelary gods and demons whose masks I saw in the dimness of the temple. This propensity does not make the Buddhists at all other-worldly. They remain quite matter-of-fact, with both feet firmly on the ground. The typical example of this full activity on two planes is the life of their greatest mystic,

Milarepa, who eight centuries ago was the most direct and practical man imaginable.

I was lucky enough to visit certain anchorites living in the silence of their cells half an hour above the village. Up there young Katche, a lama from Lhasa, had placed a winged prayer-wheel before his window, which had its paper pane tucked back: thus a continuous air-current was created which whirled the contraption. Sitting cross-legged on his earthen floor I looked at his sacred books and the pictures he had brought back from his pilgrimage to India. He showed me his tower of meditation where, like a stylite, he retired when he wished to avoid being disturbed. His nearest neighbour was a peasant from the village who had decided to live invisible and alone for three years, three months and three days. His son came every day to set food at his door. I even noticed up there that rarity, a flat piece of ground, which was surrounded by stone walls. There the hermits used to come to a kind of gymnasium for physical exercises. But there were few of these holy men left. The cells above Namche Bazar are likewise mostly empty, although lack of water may be the cause of the growing desertion there.

Wanting to find the source of the booming noise which had followed me all morning, at last I found myself in front of the house from which the great drum was sounding. From the gallery a woman cutting spinach beckoned me to go up.

It was an unforgettable moment. Seated cross-legged on the floor of a wood-panelled room, some thirty men were intoning aloud the prayers for the dead. I recognised the Tibetan Lama in his red robe and our guide Topgi. No Babu was presiding over the ceremony, seated before the ritual regalia: the thunderbolt of power which is meaningless without the bell of supreme knowledge and the manifold lamps which signify the clear light of the spirit. I sat on the floor. The sound invaded me, surrounded me, overwhelmed me.

The widow of Passang, who had been dead for a year, was the

only other woman present. She supervised a cauldron of tea into which a child would soon plunge a magnificent copper tea-pot for the benefit of the guests. The ceremony struck me as sincere and natural, for the efficacy of such occasions must inevitably depend on the attitude of the participants. On the family altar the offering cups—to the ten Buddhas, the six classes of demons and the three thousand worlds—had already been filled. For the soul of the dead in his intermediate state needs the help of both the peaceful and the terrible Buddhas. In the heart of these prayers, for those who can understand it, shines the adjuration: "The Lords of Death are your own hallucinations. . . ."

The windows of the room were carefully closed to keep in the spirits evoked and, as the day progressed, the magic incantation grew in intensity. In the smoky atmosphere I saw that by each bowl of tea burned a small butter-lamp. In the meantime I had spent several hours in the temple square where the women of the village were enjoying the funeral feast.

These expensive rites gain great prestige for the family of the deceased, whereas weddings and births are celebrated much more simply. In 1953 a Sherpa of Khumbu spent about 8,000 *rupees*—some £400—feasting his friends for several days at a family funeral.

In the temple square each female guest had produced from her coat her Tibetan bowl, in which she received in turn the beer, the rice-brandy made in the district and the *tsampa*. Finally big baskets of rice with spiced spinach and buffalo meat—which I found extremely tough—were sent round. However, when one is busy filming absorbing scenes and one is really hungry, one will eat anything!

These mourners were all women, whereas the incantators had all been men. Most of them were clean and handsome with thick, well-plaited, black hair. They all wore a golden pendant in the middle of their necklaces; they were bare-headed since the Tibetan hat with ear-flaps was too hot at that time of year. Babies in their baskets and long-haired dogs gobbled *tsampa* clumsily and amused the rest of the company. These mountain people love to laugh and have a tremendous sense of humour.

The headman told me that there is a three-week-long harvest festival in mid-July, during which 2,000 *rupees* are spent from a communal fund to which everyone contributes according to his means.

One evening, when I had agreed to give ten *rupees* for drinks, they were willing to dance for me. They tried to make me believe that the girls were so shy that they could get them to dance the Sherpa Round only after dark.

Like an immense centipede, kicking up the dust, the endless round circled, the rhythm punctuated by an onomatopœtic "*tsheu-tsheu* . . ." Arm in arm they danced, all the boys leading the slowly revolving circle. The wallflowers sat in the middle until a dancer pulled one by the arm, making her tag on to the queue. Everyone sang a familiar tune, improvising amusing words in which I was mentioned. The powerful chorus invoked the magician with "*Sseu-sseu-sseu! Phombo sseu . . . !*" with an overflowing vigour and gaiety.

It was very late and I longed to sleep, for I had decided to leave at dawn, but I was told: "You begged us to dance. Now that we are enjoying ourselves, how can you want us to stop?" The rhythm took on a vibrant life of its own, seeming to hypnotise the dancers. Voices and laughter fused, combining with the flapping prayer-flags in patterned counterpoint. Later, Katche Lama and the two nuns who were his neighbours in the high-perched hermitage got ready for their climb, lighting from the embers the bundles of bamboo which were their torches.

Katche Lama's eyes shone as we spoke of Milarepa, whose writings and songs he knew well. Milarepa spent a long time in a cave in the district of Helmo, where Malemchi is situated. Born near the Tibetan village of Kyerong, four days from where we were, he gave up his activities as a magician to become a poet and an ascetic famous in Mahayana Buddhism. Later he went to live in the Chubar Cave, just north of Mount Everest. In spite of the many privations he undertook in penance, he died aged eighty-four in 1136.

Although we doubtless understood the lines differently, I think that the young lama loved as I do these lines by Milarepa, composed when he refused to answer the questions put to him by a pretentious *pandit* (a scholar learned in the sacred texts).

> "Accustomed long to contemplating Love and Pity,
> I have forgot all difference between myself and others.
> "Accustomed long to meditating on my *Guru** as enhaloed o'er my head,
> I have forgot all those who rule by power and by prestige.
> "Accustomed as I have been to meditating on this life and the future life as one,
> I have forgot the dread of birth and death.
> "Accustomed long to regard my fleshly body as my hermitage,
> I have forgot the ease and comfort of retreats in monasteries.
> "Accustomed long to know the meaning of the Wordless,
> I have forgot the way to trace the roots of verbs and source of words and phrases."

W. Y. Evans-Wentz, *Milarepa*.
(O.U.P., 1928.)

* *Guru* means Master.

TO THE GOSAINKUND

EVER since I had been in Nepal, I had longed to go as far as the Gosainkund, the sacred Lake of the Religious, near the Tibetan frontier to the north of a pass some 15,000 feet high. Thousands of pilgrims go there in August when the snow has melted and the monsoon is in full swing. So as not to give offence to the religious authorities, the Government of Nepal has hitherto refused permission to Westerners to make this journey. But now it was only May and, if I just went, surely no one would mind. The lake would still be frozen, it was true, so I would not be able to see whether Siva really does sleep below the waters as the legend says. Luckily no one had told my interpreter to prevent my going there!

The lake was three days' journey north of Tarkhe over two passes. It was there that Siva—burning with fever after he had drunk the world's poison when the gods churned the Ocean of Milk to make the Elixir of Life—struck the rock with his trident, the conqueror of the three worlds. Three springs gushed forth from it, forming the lake which cured the god.

Our smiling guide Topgi often climbed that way in summer when he went to buy sheep in Kyerong, quite near Kyanga Tsa where Milarepa was born. Our seven porters, whose bare feet would freeze in the snow, would wait for us in the shelter of Thare Pati, where we camped high above the forest. The sergeant lent Topgi his heavy shoes so that the Sherpa could guide me on the expedition.

During the evening Topgi told a popular story about the pilgrimage to the Lake of the Religious. "Once upon a time there was a king who was building his palace at Bhadgaon. But he toiled in vain. For every night a pig pulled it to pieces again. Two soldiers set to watch told the king what happened. Fully armed, the king in his turn kept watch, saw the pig and tried to kill it, but in vain. Followed by the king, the pig fled as far as the Gosainkund, where it finally vanished. That is why, during the August full moon, the inhabitants of Bhadgaon walk as far as that lake, which is the fifth of a group hidden in these hills. Under its icy waters there lives a huge serpent, the terror of the pilgrims. At night priests and necromancers make as much noise as they can to frighten the monster. Once a magician of the Gole Tamang tribe said to his wife, 'I'll deal with that dragon on condition that you are not afraid when I bring him home.' However, when the husband came back as he had said with the subjugated monster, the terrified woman fled. Then the serpent killed the man. Since then no member of the Gole Tamang has ever joined the pilgrimage."

As soon as the tale was over, the coolies started to sing and dance the Round Dance of the previous evening. One of them was so carried away that he went into a sort of fit, muttering and trembling as if he were possessed. The others laughed and said that it was all pretence.

In the chill of the morning we embarked on the precipitous path which seemed to me to be devoid of all sense, for nine times we went down rocky spurs and nine times we went up again. (Incidentally, it is advisable to cut one's toe-nails before careering over such tracks !) I think that I would have given up if I had not been the leader of the expedition. Instead I tried to think of myself as a pilgrim, for whom this path would serve as penance.

"I take pity of the mind which cannot free itself from its
selfishness in the town set afire by the flames of desire.

"I take pity of beings in the three worlds who, wherever they
look, see no way out in the endless fire of existence.

"Alas! all the misery of transmigration,
Pity, Pity, how to heal it?"

(Tshrimedkundan.)

Topgi knew only one word of English, 'good', and each time I caught up with him I indicated the path, saying most emphatically "No good"! In the sand, newly freed from the winter snow, I saw the tracks of the rare musk-deer. It was easy to recognise the gorgeous pheasants which rocketed down from each new ravine as we entered it. At last we reached the bottom of a wild gully where we passed the night in a snowstorm. It was dry in my tiny tent, but Topgi and my tent-coolie, who was to wait for us here, sheltered against a rock-wall and burned without scruple the thin tree-trunks which bridged the mountain stream.

With the dawn I began an ascent which at this height left me breathless, under the deep blue of an absolutely clear sky. The climb had to be completed before the hot air, coming every day from India, muffled the view. I tried, but in vain, to bolster up my courage by telling myself that I would probably be the first European to see the Gosainkund.

No sooner had I reached the pass and seen the 23,000-foot summits of the Langtang Lirung which mark the Tibetan border than I threw myself violently back to avoid the paralysing cold. I put on all the clothes I had with me. The cataract of icy air which was pouring out of the north sounded like a raging demon determined to pierce all obstacles. The Sherpas call this place the Pass of Death, Balmu Sissah, because inadequately clad pilgrims, even in summer, often die from a sudden onslaught of pneumonia.

Sometimes I plunged thigh-deep in snow-drifts, sometimes I slithered over hard sections of névé-snow, compact and slowly turning to ice, so that Topgi later would tell how I was able to fly on snow. At last I saw, far below, the grey armour of the frozen lake. At its farther end it seemed to be dammed by a natural barrage, an astonishing ledge hanging between heaven and earth.

Some bamboo poles indicated the miraculous sin-remitting spring. We quenched our thirst and Topgi filled his gourd with sacred water to take home with him.

Only a lake of clear, calm waters can reflect an immutable peak or the infinite heaven, both symbols of perfection. For initiates the lake stands for the world of thought, the mind, which can only apprehend the absolute when it has become clear and calm.

Here the fevered mind of Siva, who had drunk the poison of the world, mastered itself at last by concentrating every thought on the peace of this ineffable lake, goal and crown of that inner pilgrimage which alone is the true one.

BODHNATH

SOMETIMES Buddhists join the worshippers of Siva who visit the Gosainkund. But usually they prefer to go to the great sanctuaries of 'Nepal'—as they call the valley of Kathmandu—unless they can reach as far as India and Sarnath, where the Buddha first preached, or Budh Gaya, the scene of his final enlightenment.

It is said that, already three centuries before our era, Asoka, Emperor of India and a convert to Buddhism, went on pilgrimage to Nepal, the birthplace of the Buddha. Four *stupas*, a kind of tumulus, erected by him can still be seen in the town of Patan.

Surrounded by houses, the tower of the Mahabodhi temple —a small replica of Budh Gaya built by the scholar Abhaya Raja in the sixteenth century—rises in the heart of Patan. Little niches in its truncated pyramidal tower hold five thousand statuettes of the Buddha. When I went there, Dhekye Tsering, the mother of the Dalai Lama, had just passed, and I saw her Tibetan signature in the golden book of the temple. Three days previously she had made an offering of 5,000 *rupees*—about £250—to the holy place of Bodhnath, the most important Tibetan sanctuary outside Tibet.

The white hemisphere of Bodhnath is unforgettable, with its high golden spire on which are painted the haunting blue eyes of the Primordial Buddha. A strange black sign takes the place of a nose. It is not a question-mark, as it might appear to a Westerner, for such a sign does not exist in asiatic alphabets. It is the number 'one' in Sanskrit and the symbol of power used in

China and Central Asia, representing in addition the lightning and the life-giving rains—the *lei-wen*.

The Lama of Bodhnath used to receive his many visitors on the first storey of a house facing the *stupa*. He touched the heads of the pilgrims who came "to take the dust from his feet" and to bring him offerings. He had two wives whom I met and a daughter whom he had sent by plane to Calcutta and Darjeeling to the English Convent of St. Joseph. There, as I learned from a letter in which she described her many activities, she played hockey twice a week. The Lama himself had studied in Lhasa. He was known locally as the Chini Lama because his grandfather, born in China, had finally settled down in Nepal. He had an imperious manner with his entourage and wore the traditional robe of yellow Chinese satin, but when he crossed his legs I saw the grey flannel of European trousers.

In the Buddhist temple close at hand, on a night of the full moon, I watched the ceremony of the Thousand Offerings, the gift of a Buddhist who had lost his son in the last uprising in Kathmandu. The statues of the sacred trinity—the Buddha, the Church and the Doctrine—adorned the main altar. On the walls frescoes given a warm glow by time and smoke depicted the Buddhist pantheon. At nightfall the many butter-lamps would be lit. I saw many hundreds of cups of holy water, of flour, of rice and of thin conical cakes. In a corner close to the seat of the Lama, beside the conches, the *sahnais*—a kind of oboe—and the other musical instruments of the temple, the eternal flame burned in a huge cauldron of clarified butter.

From the door of the temple I could see the great bamboo poles which denote a holy place, the treble platform with its sharp angles under the huge white *stupa*, and the thirteen degrees of the spire, symbolising the thirteen paradises which the liberated soul must transcend. From the top of the spire, surmounted by the royal parasol, garlands of tiny prayer-flags descended to the earth. Pilgrims circumambulated the sanctuary clockwise, in the direction that brings good luck. *Stupas*, which are called *chortens* in Tibetan, can contain hidden relics or offerings. Their significance is explained by W. Y. Evans-Wentz. "Exoterically it symbolises the five elements into which man's body is resolved after death. The square and solid basis stands for the earth; the globular part for the water; the spire, triangular like a flame, for the fire; the crescent, like the inverted vault of the sky, for the air; the circle, tapering in flames into space, the ether. Esoterically it symbolises the Way to Enlightenment, from the Earth through the thirteen Heavens (the thirteen segments of its spire) to the Unformed, Uncreated, whither the flame, the sacred Light of the Buddha, points and is lost in the Void." (*Milarepa*. O.U.P.)

A low wall containing prayer-wheels encircled the immense dome. Beyond it were dwelling-houses where the pilgrims might lodge. There a worker in fine metals made ritual objects which were bought by long-haired hillmen from distant valleys.

This extraordinary tumulus, at least fifteen centuries old, is supposed to have been built in expiation of an involuntary parricide. But the Tibetans, who favour it most, explain its origin otherwise. They say that a tear of pity fell from the eyes of Avalokitesvara and from it was born a heavenly maiden. This young creature was tempted to steal the flowers of paradise and, in punishment, she was debased to be born into a swineherd's family in Nepal. Later she was married and became rich raising geese. She decided to devote her fortune to building a religious monument, and therefore begged the king to give her the amount of ground that could be covered by a sheepskin. The king agreed. She then took a skin and cut it into very thin strips, which she used to mark out a considerable area. The worried ministers urged the king to intervene but, honouring his word, he allowed her to proceed. The foundress died before she achieved her object, but her sons were able to finish the building. Inside it they put certain relics of the Buddha Kasyapa. As a reward they were reborn in Tibet, where one of them adapted the Tibetan alphabet from the Sanskrit and the other became the first Tibetan abbot. The elephant which had been used to transport the building materials, enraged at having been left out of the rewards, resolved on vengeance. He became the King Glan Darma, a fanatical enemy of Buddhism. However, the last of the three brothers became the Lama Phal Dorje, who in A.D. 902 killed Glan Darma.

The Chini Lama told me this story in his own very individual English. He said that it would be mimed in the Demons' Dance which we were about to see. The peasant actors had dressed up and were adjusting their heavy carved masks—the colours of which indicate the various classes of demons which are the evil forces within us.

The dance was led by the magician in a huge black hat covered with startling symbols; they included the mirror in which the demons, summoned by the power of the magician, see themselves, lose their strength and are forced to obey their master. Water monsters supported Death, as well as the circle of the universe and the victorious thunderbolt of the Buddha. Bunches of ribbon in the five primary colours, denoting the five elements, formed the centre of the hat.

The orchestra produced overpowering sounds through the whole range of the scale. There were two huge trumpets rather like Alpine horns, except that they were telescopic and made of copper and silver. In addition there were the conches which sound through the 3,000 worlds, the huge drum hit by a curved stick, the human thigh-bone made into a flute to govern the demons, and the *sahnais*, a kind of oboe which is rinsed with water in the intervals when the weather is very hot. Cymbals emphasised the rhythm, together with the ritual bell, shaken by the Lama wonderfully hatted in a brocade mitre decorated with embossed Buddhas. The ogre, a boy whose belly was tattooed in blue, wore a full wig made of yak-tails.

The dance mimed how Lama Phal Dorje, the third son of the

foundress of the temple, reborn as a magician, transformed himself into a dancing camel and succeeded in killing the wicked Tibetan king with an arrow shot through a key-hole! Once the king was dead, it was discovered that he had the horns and black tongue of a demon. And that is why the Tibetan peasants you meet on mountain-paths greet you with a pinkly protruding tongue, to show that they have nothing devilish about them!

SVAYAMBHU

THE most ancient Buddhist sanctuary in Nepal, where men have come to worship for twenty-three centuries, is Svayambhu—the Self-Existing-One. Reached by three hundred steps, it crowns a hill rising not far from Kathmandu.

This *stupa* was built at the spot where once blazed the Jewel in the miraculous lotus, a spontaneous manifestation of the divine at a time when man's vision was not obscured by ignorance. Around its foothills stand statues of the Buddha, calling the earth to witness to the virtues by right of which he occupies the throne of the supreme victory. They recall the moment when Mara, the Evil One, vainly challenged the Buddha.

When I reached the top of the hill I found it alive and swirling with sound: gongs, bells, monkeys picking up rice-offerings, sacrificial fires sizzling, different sets of 108 butter-lamps to be made ready, priests mechanically reciting the offices for the faithful above the *mandala*, the magic circle of the universe. Round the white dome—symbol of the Womb of Creation—processed Newars, Sherpas, narrow-eyed Tibetans, all carrying trays of flowers and rice.

At the four cardinal points of the dome were niches, each containing an altar surmounted by a Buddha in meditation to whom the pilgrims threw rice. A guardian prevented me from raising a curtain of bronze flowers which protected Amitabha, the Buddha of infinite compassion whose chapel is the most revered of all. A peacock, the bird dedicated to Amitabha, made of gilded bronze glowed from the top of a stone column. Beside it smiled the good goddess Tara, holding in her hand the stalk of the miraculous lotus. She is to be the wife of the next Buddha.

As at Bodhnath, the white tumulus is crowned by a square structure supporting the spire, the *toran*, which has the eyes of the Buddha on each of its four sides. The unforgettable gaze of the Primordial Buddha reminded me of the dreaming Buddha of the far-off Bayon of Angkor. Here the thirteen storeys of the spire are made of superimposed sections and not of stepped degrees as at Bodhnath, but here, too, a parasol surmounts the whole, symbol of the sovereign divine law.

The atmosphere at Svayambhu was alive with devotion, despite the children playing hide-and-seek and the families camping in the corners of the terrace. To the west of the square was a Buddhist temple. I climbed to its first floor by a steep and narrow staircase, my heart beating fast, uncertain whether I was allowed to do so. I stopped before three huge Buddhas covered with precious silks. The sacred flame, fed on butter, burned bright in a cauldron. Nepalese attendants, angered by my intrusion, came towards me with threatening looks and I prudently retired.

In a recess of the square, against a wall, stood an enormous statue of Vishnu, seeming to watch the gambling coolies absorbed in their dice. Not far away, on the threshold of the pagoda of Sitala—the Hindu goddess of smallpox—two men in white were laying an offering of sweet rice-cakes covered with flies. Here the divinities of the different religions seemed to live in as good accord as did their worshippers.

From the top of Svayambhu one can see the whole plain of Kathmandu. When Topgi visited it, he was told that the *bodhisattva* Manjusri created the valley in which Kathmandu lies. (A *bodhisattva* is the perfect or 'liberated' man who decides to enter Buddhahood only after the liberation of all living beings.) Long ago a lake filled the whole region. Passing by, the Buddha Vipasya threw a lotus seed into the water. In time it sprouted and a marvellous flower opened in the middle of the lake. It was as big as a cartwheel, its ten thousand golden petals were encrusted with diamonds and lined with pearls and its centre was of rubies. Its pollen was jewelled and its stamens were of gold. From its corolla sprang a flame, purer, more splendid and more precious than the rays of the sun. It was Adi-Buddha, the One who transcends all.

The all-knowing *bodhisattva* Manjusri knew that a spontaneous manifestation of the divine had taken place in Nepal. With his two wives he left China. He passed through the circle of mountains which imprisoned the lake to the north-east and, after three nights of contemplation, piously circumambulated the water clockwise. Then the task committed to him was revealed. With his triumphant sword, which flashed in his hand like a ray from the moon, he was to cut a passage through the mountain-barrier to release the water. He carried out the divine orders and liberated the Bagmati river, together with the *naga* monsters which lived in its depths. The bottom of the lake became visible, and with it the long stalk of the lotus carrying the Self-Existing-One in its precious flower. Manjusri approached its root respectfully. Hearing the mysterious murmur of a spring, he bowed and worshipped. Then he settled nearby on a spur of ground where today the Newars still worship the marks left by his sacred feet, which can be recognised by the eyes which adorn them! When his task was finally accomplished, he returned to his hill in China, the Wu T'ai Shan, which is said to possess relics of the Buddha.*

This story underlines the ancient ties which link China to Nepal by way of Tibet. Similarly, it was thanks to two princesses, one Nepalese and one Chinese, that Tibet became Buddhist in the seventh century. These two women, both married to the King of Tibet, converted their husband into a faithful follower of the Buddha.

The whole Buddhist world reveres the esoteric formula *aum*, which is to be seen literally at every cross-roads. It is addressed

* See Sylvain Levi: *Le Népal* (Annales du Musée Guimet).

to the first Dalai Lama, terrestrial incarnation of the *bodhisattva* Avalokitesvara. "*Aum! Mani padme hum!* Veneration to the Jewel in the lotus!" The true meaning of the sacred words must be hidden, but we curious Westerners are not at peace until everything is explained somehow. *Aum* may be taken as the symbol of the whole creation, the essence of happiness, of good fortune, of knowledge and of the great way of liberation. A start to the interpretation of these words may be made by remembering that unearthly flame born of the lotus-flower in the myth of Svayambhu, the Self-Existing-One—a magnificent name for the ultimate principle. The Jewel of immutable Reality is to be found even in the heart of the fragile mutability of a flower.

It is mainly during the winter and the spring that the Sherpas visit "Shimbu", as Svayambhu is called by the local inhabitants. It was in this incomparable place that I lived through the following scene, as I leant against a small *chaitya* or votive monument.

A slender, broad-shouldered man had just reached the top of the three hundred steps. His straight nose, the proud arch of his eyebrows and his long hair showed him to be a Hindu, while the flame-coloured cloth in which he was draped denoted the *sannyasin*—a religious beggar who has renounced the world. I had thought of him in the guise of a Greek tragedian until I saw his clear eyes, overflowing with a calm joy.

He walked in a leisurely way around the great *stupa*, showing no interest in the surrounding religious activities. Was he perhaps fulfilling some old vow, the realisation of which no longer had much importance? His tour accomplished, he sat, simple and noble, on the highest step of the big staircase, away from the pilgrims and alone. There he sat for a long time, supple and vital although completely still, looking ahead but seeing nothing. There was absolute peace about him. He was a man who knew. Holy places, prayers, strivings, desires, visions of a world joyous or in torment, all were nothing but passing shadows on the unmoving screen of the Jewel, the unparalleled Self-Existing-One.

When at last he stood to go down towards the town, I had no idea how much time had gone by while his all-embracing gaze opened for me the path that leads beyond time.

Kept alive by the faith of the peasants and hill-people, Svayambhu is a vital place, syncretising the cults of Siva, of Vishnu and of the Buddha, who in the great country of Nepal are all considered one.

How long will this continue to be so?

The old customs are shaken by waves of political unrest. The frontiers are open and today foreigners can still watch the scenes of a daily life in which religion is part of every moment. But their surprise is soon replaced by anxiety as they come to see how this ancient conception of life is doomed to be replaced by a planned democracy which aims at a foundation of universal suffrage. Modern Nepal is greatly influenced by the Indian Congress, while a few of her Communist citizens have turned to Tibet and Peking for refuge.

It is true enough that during my stay in Kathmandu King Tribhuvana, the terrestrial incarnation of Vishnu, went to the sanctuary of Svayambhu on the birthday of the Lord Buddha . . . but he went in order to deliver a harangue on democracy.

Such is life in our twentieth century.

LIST OF ILLUSTRATIONS

1. THE HIGH VALLEYS

1. NEPAL HAS OPENED HER GATES. A Gurung shepherd boy, wearing homespun woven by his mother, looks out upon the world.

2. SHELTERED WITHIN THE GREAT MOUNTAINS. Beyond the gorge of the Dudh Kosi lies the valley of Khumbu, a Sherpa name which means 'sanctuary'. The Taweche looms ahead to the north, some 21,200 ft. high.

3. NAMCHE BAZAR, THE SHERPA 'CAPITAL'. Namche Bazar, a village of some sixty houses, is built at an altitude of 12,600 ft. Near it run two rivers, one coming from the foot of Everest, the other from the Nangpa La pass which leads into Tibet. Over this 19,000-ft. pass come hundreds of traders bringing wool, salt and borax to the south.

4. YAKS PLOUGHING BELOW THAMSERKU. These yaks are ploughing fields 12,000 ft. high, while the summit of Thamserku (21,730 ft.) looms beyond them. Potatoes and barley are grown wherever it is possible in the Khumbu region. The yak, *bos grognens*, is essential to Sherpa life. The hardiest of animals, it gives very rich milk, is surefooted and carries heavy loads.

5. FIELDS WON FROM THE MOUNTAIN-SIDE. In this land of mountains every field is a victory. This view of the hamlet of Teshinga, seen from Thyangboche, shows the difficulty of constructing fields in so precipitous a country.

6. A VIRGIN PEAK, HOME OF THE GODS. The astonishing Cholatse rises above the Lobuja Khola. To the Sherpas all summits are sacred, for they are the seat of the divinity.

7. YOUNG SHERPAS AT SCHOOL. Tsering Dorje teaches English to some small pupils in Namche Bazar. A smattering of English, in addition to Tibetan and Nepali, will be of great help to them in their future climbs with Europeans.

8. A SHERPA GREETING. A Sherpa woman puts out her tongue in greeting. This custom may perhaps derive from the legend of a wicked king who, after his death, was found to have the horns and black tongue of a demon. Polite Sherpas therefore want to prove that they are not descended from him.

9. A CHORTEN, THE SYMBOL OF LIFE. Behind this *chorten* can be seen the shingled roofs of the Buddhist monastery of Thyangboche. In the foreground is a row of stones engraved with the prayer, "*Aum! Mani padme hum!*" The five parts of the *chorten*, which may contain offerings or relics, stand exoterically for the five elements of which man's body is composed. Esoterically they symbolise the Way of Enlightenment which leads from the Earth through the thirteen Heavens to the Void.

10. TENZING NORKEY, MOST FAMOUS OF SHERPAS.

11. THE WATER-CARRIER. Lamo Doma, the pretty water-carrier of Namche Bazar, has the true Mongolian eye characteristic of the Sherpas. She wears a typical necklace of coral beads and *zi* stones, a kind of agate which may come from neolithic graves. The plaster on her temples is a cure for a headache.

12. HUMAN CARAVAN. Files of Tamangs, the women wearing numerous necklaces of red beads, carry their goods to the town in bamboo baskets. They are helped to bear their heavy loads by a leather belt across the forehead, while a string shoulder-strap prevents sideways slips. They walk bare-

foot, and their feet, flattened by heavy loads, are amazingly sure, travelling lightly and unerringly across dangerous scree or rocks slippery with rain or moss.

13. DISTANT MIRACLE. The summit of the Langtang Lirung (23,771 ft.) on the Tibetan border beckons with its snow-peaks. Between it and the Chiba Danda slopes, on which I stand, are many steep and forested ridges.

14. MAN'S PATIENCE. A whole mountain-side is built into terraces which sometimes bear two harvests a year : first wheat and then *gohya* rice. The last fields of the valley may be so narrow that the plough can barely make a half-turn in them.

15. DEEP ARE THE VALLEYS. The path from Malemchi plunges downwards before climbing to Tarkhe Gyang. On the left is a tree-rhododendron in blossom. On the right is a stunted Himalayan oak. Its branches have been stripped for cattle-food, leaving it almost leafless.

16. TOPGI. Topgi is sharpening a bamboo stick with his *kukri*, a curved jungle knife made of the best steel. He wears the long narrow trousers and soft cap of the Nepalese.

17. CHEESE-MAKING. A shepherd churns butter-milk to make *siri*, a name which recalls the *séré* made in the same way in Switzerland. His nailless wooden pail is just like those made in the Alps.

18. MOTHER AND CHILD. They sit in the sun on their balcony.

19. THE VILLAGE OF TARKHE. A view of Tarkhe Gyang looking north. The houses are built with shingled roofs. The entrance to the village is marked by *chortens* and a white prayer-flag flutters by each house.

20. HEADMAN'S WIFE. The wife of Buru Kanche, headman of the village, wears a Tibetan cap of felt with fur ear-flaps. A golden phylactery hangs from her necklace of turquoise and coral beads, among which can be seen the *zi* stones with their white 'eyes'. She wears her striped woollen apron at her back to protect her skirt when she sits on the ground.

21. DIGNITY. While I reload my Leica, the mother of the headman waits in a posture of natural meditation. She wears her dress for festive days, made of the best Chinese satin. The way in which the long sleeves are rolled up reminds me of the Mongol fashion.

22. BROTHER AND SISTER.

23. WINNOWING GRAIN. Topgi is husking the rye. With his foot he manipulates a hammer-headed beam which pounds the grain in a hollow. His wife winnows it with a light straw tray.

24. PRAYER UNCEASING. Katche, a lama from Lhasa who has spent two years in the hermitage of Tarkhe, explains in which direction the prayer-wheel must turn in order to bring luck. Before his window he has placed an Æolian prayer-wheel which the wind turns incessantly. Within the prayer-wheel is thin, tightly-rolled paper on which prayers, in Tibetan and Sanskrit, are written over and over again.

25. THE HUBBLE-BUBBLE. Topgi smokes a water-pipe on the balcony of the house. Behind, a neighbour carrying a cradle on her back stops to chat with his sister Lakpuri.

26. WORKING PARTY. Women gather in a lane to weave and spin wool together. Similar looms are used throughout Central Asia. A prayer-flag stands in the background.

27. CAUGHT IN A SNARE. The big red pheasant has been filled with straw and hung out to dry. All the houses in the village face south and their beautifully carved windows have three openings.

28. AT THE FOOT OF THE ALTAR. Tung Sang Lamini, a devout widow, sits at the foot of the family altar, close to the window. In her hands she has a rosary. Cups of lustral water stand before the Buddha and there is a holy book on the left of the shrine.

29. KITCHEN COMFORT. In the kitchen corner of the living-room, opposite the window, an open fire burns on a stone slab. An iron tripod stands over it and there is a drying-rack above, on which meat is being smoked. The panelled walls have many shelves and sliding cupboards, in which are provisions, spices and brass utensils. The man's bowl contains *rakshi*, a local brandy made from grain.

30. CURRYING POTATOES. Beautiful Karmu, who is nineteen and not yet married, cooks with elegant gestures. Her ear-rings are made of gold and she has some fine agates in her necklace. Behind her, on the shelves with the utensils, are all the spices which she needs for the curry.

31. BRANDY-DRINKER. Even the youngest member of the party drinks rice-brandy. He wears a shiny pink satin cap, like the red ones worn by babies in Peking. The traditionally shaped bowl is lined with silver. Such bowls are personal belongings, carried inside the coat, and if the wood comes from a maple bole can be very costly.

32. MAGIC. The boy Naropa has just placed a tray with doll-like figures made of dough on the path at the back entrance of the village. This will prevent the return of his father's illness, recently exorcised by the priest.

33. WITTY OLD WOMAN. She is 88, she lives alone and her jokes and witticisms are famous.

34. FUNERAL FEAST. Only women and children are catered for here in the temple square. The widow of Passang, who has been dead for a year, has provided millet-beer, *rakshi* and buttered

tea. To eat, there is *tsampa* and baskets of rice with spiced spinach and buffalo meat. In the foreground a woman nurses her baby in a covered cradle.

35. PREPARING TSAMPA. *Tsampa* is the bread of the high valleys. Each guest prepares her own, kneading the roasted barley flour into the buttered tea in her own bowl. All these charming women wear golden ear-rings. They have golden pendants hanging from their necklaces, and are clean and handsome, with thick, plaited, black hair.

36. PRAYER FOR THE DEAD. In the room of the dead man, Passang, the long ritual prayers are succeeded by traditional music. This is played on the huge drum and the long horns. No Babu, in the background, shakes the sacred bell, signifying supreme knowledge. Also included in the ritual regalia are the thunderbolt of power and the lamps denoting the light of the spirit. The wicks of the butter-lamps are alight beside every bowl of tea and before the family altar, and the paper panes of the window are shut.

37. THE DEMONS WITHIN US. These demon masks, their hair made of yaks' tails, are kept in the temple and used at religious festivals. Their different colours correspond to the various forces of evil within man which must be propitiated. Their size indicates plainly that demons are stronger than man and that man therefore needs the help of the magician to master them.

38. SACRED TWILIGHT OF THE TEMPLE. The temple of Tarkhe Gyang, with its gilded and lacquered pillars, is lit only from the door. Like most Nepalese temples, it has been decorated by itinerant Tibetan artists. The three sacred Buddhas are seated on lotuses above the altar; before them are offerings of water, rice and lights. To the right can be seen four huge books belonging to the sacred Kanjur; on the left is the great drum.

39. WHEEL OF TEN MILLION PRAYERS. Topgi pushes the big drum of the temple prayer-wheel, decorated with mediæval Nepalese

characters. The small bell hanging from the ceiling is rung by each revolution of the cylinder.

40. SHERPA ROUND DANCE. On the slightest pretext the Sherpas gather to drink, sing and dance their special Round Dance after sunset. The boys lead the slow shuffling while everybody sings. The wallflowers sit in the middle, waiting to be pulled into the round. In the background, prayer-flags rise around the village square.

41. THE WAY OF PILGRIMAGE. From Thare Pati, the Steep Shelter, the pilgrims' way plunges to the bottom of the rugged slope. Then it reaches upwards to the Pass of Death, Balmu Sissah as the Sherpas call it, where the icy wind from the north attacks the faithful.

42. THE SACRED LAKE. The goal of the pilgrimage is the fifth lake, the Gosainkund, which is still frozen. Behind it, to the north-west, the Ganesh Himal reaches 22,250 ft. The five lakes are called Helmo, Norcho, Serzho, Nkunlzo and Chu. Beneath the waters of the sacred lake lies Siva, cured of his fever, who with his trident created the sacred spring. Alone in the wild valley, we are the first pilgrims of the year.

2. PLACES OF PILGRIMAGE

43. THE SANCTUARIES AWAIT PILGRIMS. The sanctuaries of Nepal attract many Buddhists from the mountains, from Tibet, from India and from Burma.

44. THE DURBAR SQUARE OF PATAN. In the Durbar Square of Patan, founded in the year A.D. 630, pagodas of carved wood stand beside the Hindu temple of Radhakrishna, built of stone in 1637. Sheltered beneath a cobra's hood, the king Yogendra Malla prays on the top of a stone pillar—a typical Nepalese monument.

45. THE MAHABODHI TEMPLE. In Patan the pilgrim visits the Mahabodhi Temple, with its niches containing many hundreds of small figures of Buddha. Built by Abhaja Raja, a sixteenth-century scholar, it is a modest replica of the famous Budh Gaya of Bihar, where the Buddha attained self-realisation. (The Wu Ta Tze in Peking was inspired by this monument.)

46. KIRTIPUR, TOWN OF GLORY. The pilgrim climbs this hill to reach the *stupas* of Chillandeo, where he sees the eyes of Adi Buddha, the Primordial One. Here the Newars, in 1768, resisted the Gurkha invasion for two years.

47. BODHNATH: THE EYES OF WISDOM. "The eyes of wisdom see throughout eternity the realms of light." The unforgettable white hemisphere of Bodhnath, with its golden spire on which are painted the haunting blue eyes of the Primordial Buddha, has been an important place of pilgrimage since the fifth century. The top of the spire, with the parasol of the Law, is nearly 150 ft. high. Surrounded by a low wall carrying prayer-wheels, the dome rests on a treble star-shaped platform. The thirteen steps of the spire stand for the thirteen Heavens of the Way to Liberation, and the Buddha's third eye represents transcendental knowledge. The sign in place of a nose is the numeral one in Sanskrit—a symbol of power throughout Central Asia.

48. THE THOUSAND OFFERINGS. The Lama of Bodhnath—the Chini Lama—is about to start the ceremony of the Thousand Offerings—fire, water, rice, flour and *torma*, cones made of dough, butter and sugar. The sacred triad of Buddhas stands over the altar and the Buddhist pantheon is depicted in frescoes on the walls. The butter-lamps are not yet lit, but the eternal flame burns perpetually in the huge cauldron of clarified butter beside the Lama.

49. TIBETAN ORCHESTRA. This orchestra accompanies the Demons' Dance, and includes horns made of copper and silver, drums, cymbals, conches and *sahnais*, a kind of oboe.

50. THE CHINI LAMA. The Chini Lama, so called because his grandfather came from China, belongs to the oldest Buddhist order which permits marriage. He wears the traditional dress of yellow satin and holds the double drum and the bell, symbol of the supreme Void. Topping the headdress of his order, the thunderbolt denotes the power of the Buddha.

51. NEPALESE SAGE. Holding a small double drum, this dignified peasant wears a rosary round his neck.

52. DEMONS AT REST. Beside the white elephant which faces the temple, the dancers rest. They wear heavy wooden masks. The five small skulls which they wear for diadems are proof of the Tantric influence on Tibetan Buddhism: they stand for the Five Poisons of mortal life which must become the Five Wisdoms of eternal life.

53. BLACK-HAT MAGICIAN. He wears the traditional hat to lead the Demons' Dance. The mirror on its crown will reflect the arrival of the demons whom he summons. The water-monsters, or *makaras*, supporting it denote life and fertility. In the middle of the circle of the universe is the thunderbolt, master of death symbolised by a skull. The thunderbolt also rules over the five elements, which are indicated by the knots of ribbon in five colours.

54. A KING AND HIS TWO QUEENS. At the entrance to Kathmandu, the capital of Nepal, King Pratapa Malla and his two wives look out over the Himalayas. In 1661 this king received at his court two Jesuit fathers, arriving from Tibet and China. Now he sits motionless as a crow takes flight from the shoulder of one of his queens.

55. WORSHIPPER OF VISHNU. In the Durbar Square stands a magnificent seventeenth-century statue of Garuda, mythical king of the birds, with his powerful eagle wings. His serpent necklace recalls the truce made between Garuda and the King of the Snakes. Garuda is the vehicle of Vishnu.

56. ANNAPURNA'S TEMPLE. The temple of Annapurna is a golden-roofed pagoda in old Kathmandu. The name of the capital is derived from the Sanskrit *kastha mandapa*—wooden hall. The copper ribbon which hangs from the top of the temple is a snake-god symbol, signifying the eternal underground powers. Annapurna herself is an aspect of Shakti, the supreme energy, when she grants the fulfilment of spiritual or material needs.

57. BHAIRAVA AND THE CHILD. Religious life is not separate from ordinary life; they are one. Gods may be worshipped in the midst of the traffic without self-consciousness.

58. RAVANA WITH THE TEN HEADS. The king of the demons is a figure in a wedding procession.

59. DEVOTIONS. At Badhpatinath a worshipper places *curcuma*, a red powder consecrated by the priest, on his head. Beautifully chased panels of gilded bronze, such as this one, are to be seen everywhere. On this example the usual door-keepers, the *makaras*, are clearly to be seen, as well as the *nagas*, the princes of the serpents, who symbolise the underground energy.

60. THE PEDICURE. At the foot of a pagoda, an old woman paints a young girl's toes with purple liquid.

61. THE HEART OF KATHMANDU. The royal pagoda, built in 1549, rises above nine terraces. It is consecrated to Taleju, an aspect of Devi, who helped King Harisimha to conquer Nepal in 1325. The royal pagoda is used thirty-six times in a year.

62. CLEAR WATER OF THE PRANALIS. Those who want to acquire merit may present a town with public fountains or *pranalis* such as this one. Bronze or stone spouts depict the *makaras*, the vehicles of the river-goddess Ganga.

63. TEMPLE OF RADHAKRISHNA. In Nepal it is still possible to see how the very old wooden architecture influenced the later stone monuments.

64. CARVING IN A BASANTAPUR COURT. Such magnificent woodwork can be found all over Kathmandu.

65. THE PASSAGE OF THE GOD. April is the time of the New Year festival, when the sacred car of Matsyendra, the rain god, is pulled around the city by his devotees. The Small Matsyendra is a piece of white wood. The cult was introduced by King Narendra Deva in the eighth century. The Nepalese throng the square and, as the god passes, try to touch the sacred car or obtain a flower from the priests. Women remain in the background. There is no hostility towards me or my camera.

66. PROCESSIONAL CART. The three eyes of the deity are painted on the wheels of this small processional cart, photographed in Bhatgaon. In the background two ceremonial parasols shelter sedan-chairs in which a bride and bridegroom are going to their wedding.

67. PRIESTS OF THE BHAVANI TEMPLE. Priests of the Bhavani Temple in Harisiddhi still wear the old and rare Nepalese costume.

68. MAHAKALA—BENEFICENT BUT TERRIBLE. In the middle of the Durbar Square stands Mahakala. Usually called 'the Great Black', he is a Nepalese aspect of Siva symbolising the Great Time, 'the swallower of the ages'. One of his six hands holds the *trishula* or trident. The trident, master of the three worlds—earth, air and ether, or the world of forms, the formless world and the subtle world—is also the emblem of the Buddha and indicates sacred ground. The double drum of Siva symbolises creation, which started out of the Void in response to primordial sound. His necklace is made of the heads of his devotees; sun and moon obey him and his foot crushes ignorance. At his feet sits a Brahmin priest.

69. SIVA, GOD OF ANNIHILATION. This Siva *bhairab* in gilded wood rests on a tortoise, symbol of preservation. It is coloured in gold, black, red and white. By it crouch the priest and his daughter, beside the ritual objects.

70. THE BUDDHA CALLS THE EARTH TO WITNESS. Around the foothills which lead to the sanctuary of Svayambhu are statues of the Buddha calling the earth to witness to the virtues by right of which he occupies the Supreme Throne. Three hundred steps lead to the *stupa*, goal of pilgrimages for twenty-three centuries. A legend makes the holy place older still, saying that it was created by Prachanda Deva, a king from Bengal who came to Nepal as a religious beggar.

71. BUDDHA OF INFINITE COMPASSION. Serene and radiant, Amitabha, Buddha of infinite compassion, smiles from behind a curtain of bronze flowers.

72. AWAITING THE OFFERINGS. Four niches, sheltering Buddhas, are built into the round *stupa* which crowns the famous hill. Pilgrims throw grain and flowers at the feet of the Buddha, and there a monkey waits for offerings of rice.

73. PRIEST AND PILGRIM. Sitting before the round *mandala* of the universe, a priest chants prayers for the pilgrim beside him. In the square bronze frame are made the offerings to Fire, the pure messenger of the gods. On the temple an inscription reads: "I bow to the Buddha, I bow to the Church, I bow to the Law."

74. THE SHRINE OF SITALA. On the threshold of the pagoda of Sitala, the Hindu goddess of smallpox, the pilgrims have placed an offering of sweet rice-cakes, covered with flies, and flowers. Now they pour lustral water under the direction of the priest.

75. TARA THE COMPASSIONATE. Tara the Compassionate will be the wife of the coming Buddha. She is the equal of the *bodhisattvas*, she is the Saviour. Once her hand held a lotus. The statue and the halo are of gilded bronze, for the Nepalese have been famous for centuries for their skill in casting bronze.

76. BRAHMIN PRIEST. This Brahmin priest at Budha Nilkantha wears the rosaries sacred to Siva and Vishnu, the *rudraksha* beads and

the cowries. Budha Nilkantha means 'Old Blue Throat'. This is a name given to Siva and indicates that the place was formerly dedicated to him.

77. ROYAL FOUNTAIN. This beautiful fountain is at Balaji, near the small Vishnu lying upon the waters.

78. VISHNU UPON THE WATERS. All pilgrims visit the park of Balaji where this statue was set in the seventeenth century by King Pratapa Malla, when he 'heard' that the god would kill him if he went to the great Budha-Nilkantha Vishnu for his devotions. Vishnu, the Soul of the Universe, the All-Pervading, sleeps peacefully on the formless waters on the coils of the snake Ananta, the Endless One, Eternal Time.

The author's photographs were taken with a Leica camera.

The author is grateful for permission to use the following photographs:

Nos. 1, 2, 3, 5, 6, 7, 8, 9 and 11. Foundation for Alpine Researches.

No. 4. Professor Christoph von Fürer-Haimendorf.

No. 10. Ludwig Krenek.

THE PICTURES

Part One

THE HIGH VALLEYS

1–42

Part Two

PLACES OF PILGRIMAGE

43–78

1 NEPAL HAS OPENED HER GATES

2 SHELTERED WITHIN THE GREAT MOUNTAINS

3 NAMCHE BAZAR, THE SHERPA "CAPITAL"

4 YAKS PLOUGHING BELOW THAMSERKU

5 FIELDS WON FROM THE MOUNTAIN-SIDE

6 A VIRGIN PEAK, HOME OF THE GODS

7 YOUNG SHERPAS AT SCHOOL

8 A SHERPA GREETING

9 A CHORTEN, THE SYMBOL OF LIFE

10 TENZING NORKEY, MOST FAMOUS OF SHERPAS

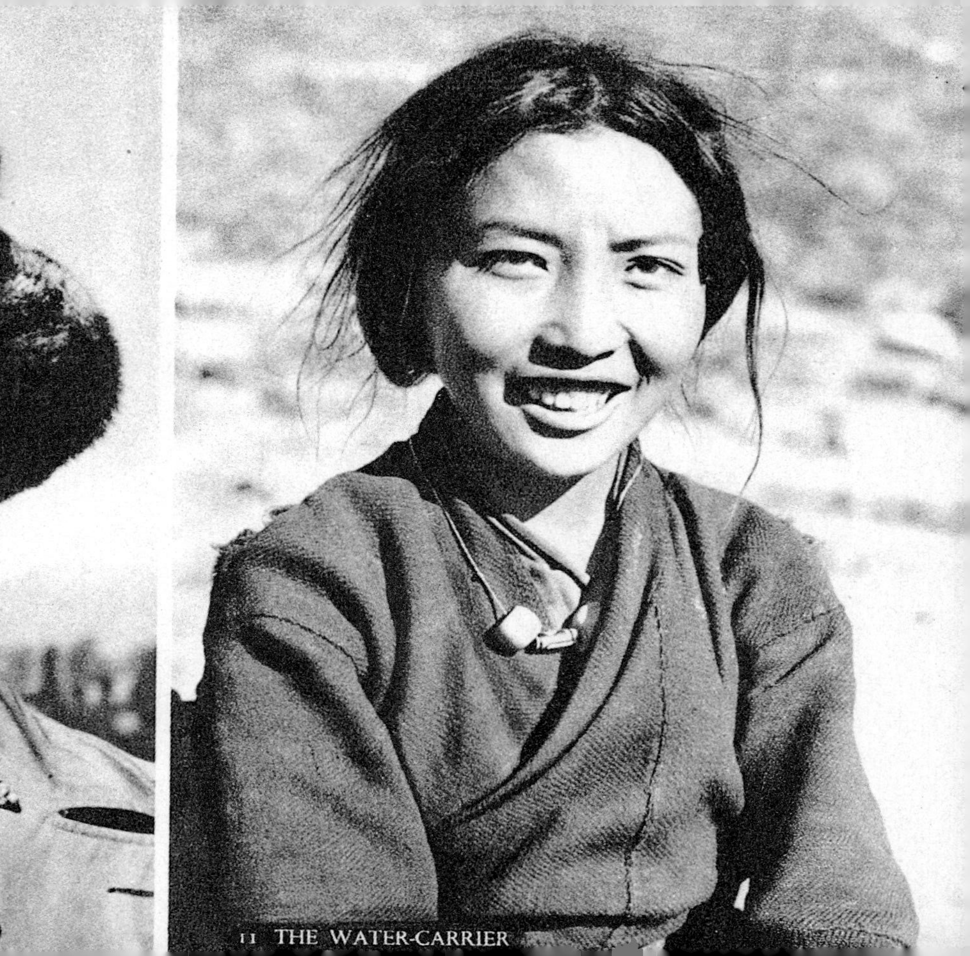

11 THE WATER-CARRIER

12 HUMAN CARAVAN

13 DISTANT MIRACLE

14 MAN'S PATIENCE

15 DEEP ARE THE VALLEYS

16 TOPGI

17 CHEESE-MAKING

18 MOTHER AND CHILD

19 THE VILLAGE OF TARKHE

20 HEADMAN'S WIFE

21 DIGNITY

22 BROTHER AND SISTER

23 WINNOWING GRAIN

24 PRAYER UNCEASING

27 THE HUBBLE-BUBBLE

26 WORKING PARTY

27 CAUGHT IN A SNARE

28 AT THE FOOT OF THE ALTAR

29 KITCHEN COMFORT

30 CURRYING POTATOES

31 BRANDY-DRINKER

32 MAGIC

33 WITTY OLD WOMAN

34 FUNERAL FEAST

35 PREPARING TSAMPA

36 PRAYER FOR THE DEAD

37 THE DEMONS WITHIN US

38 SACRED TWILIGHT OF THE TEMPLE

39 WHEEL OF TEN MILLION PRAYERS

40 SHERPA ROUND DANCE

41 THE WAY OF PILGRIMAGE

42 THE SACRED LAKE

43 THE SANCTUARIES AWAIT PILGRIMS

44 THE DURBAR SQUARE OF PATAN

45 THE MAHABODHI TEMPLE

46 KIRTIPUR, TOWN OF GLORY

47 BODHNATH : THE EYES OF WISDOM

48 THE THOUSAND OFFERINGS

19 TIBETAN ORCHESTRA

50 THE CHINI LAMA

51 NEPALESE SAGE

52 DEMONS AT REST

53 BLACK HAT MAGICIAN

54 A KING AND HIS TWO QUEENS

55 WORSHIPPER OF VISHNU

56 ANNAPURNA'S TEMPLE

57 SHAIRAVA AND THE CHILD

58 RAVANA WITH THE TEN HEADS

59 DEVOTIONS

60 THE PEDICURE

61 THE HEART OF KATHMANDU

62 CLEAR WATER OF THE PRANALIS

63 TEMPLE OF RADHAKRISHNA

64 CARVING IN A BASANTAPUR COURT

65 THE PASSAGE OF THE GOD

66 PROCESSIONAL CART

67 PRIESTS OF THE BHAVANI TEMPLE

68 MAHAKALA—BENEFICENT BUT TERRIBLE

69 SIVA, GOD OF ANNIHILATION

70 THE BUDDHA CALLS THE EARTH TO WITNESS

71. BUDDHA OF INFINITE COMPASSION

72 AWAITING THE OFFERINGS

73 PRIEST AND PILGRIM

74 THE SHRINE OF SITALA

75 TARA THE COMPASSIONATE

76 BRAHMIN PRIEST

77 ROYAL FOUNTAIN

78 VISHNU UPON THE WATERS